OF NATURE

WORDSWORTH'S POETRY ON NATURE

By

WILLIAM WORDSWORTH

This edition is published by Ragged Hand,
an imprint of Read & Co.

British Library Cataloguing-in-Publication Data
A catalogue record for this book is available from the British Library.

Read & Co. is part of Read Books Ltd.
For more information visit
www.readandcobooks.co.uk

CONTENTS

William Wordsworth

"Mr. Wordsworth . . . had a dignified manner, with a deep and roughish but not unpleasing voice, and an exalted mode of speaking.

He had a habit of keeping his left hand in the bosom of his waistcoat; and in this attitude, except when he turned round to take one of the subjects of his criticism from the shelves (for his contemporaries were there also), he sat dealing forth his eloquent but hardly catholic judgments. . . . Walter Scott said that the eyes of Burns were the finest he ever saw. I cannot say the same of Mr. Wordsworth; that is, not in the sense of the beautiful, or even of the profound. But certainly I never beheld eyes which looked so inspired and supernatural.

They were like fires half burning, half smouldering with a sort of acrid fixture of regard, and seated at the further end of two caverns. One might imagine Ezekiel or Isaiah to have had such eyes.

The finest eyes, in every sense of the word,

which I have ever seen in a man's head (and I have seen many fine ones), are those of Thomas Carlyle."—1815.

AN EXCERPT FROM
The Autobiography of Leigh Hunt, 1850

"His features were large, and not suddenly expressive; they conveyed little idea of the 'poetic fire' usually associated with brilliant imagination. His eyes were mild and up-looking, his mouth coarse rather than refined, his forehead high rather than broad; but every action seemed considerate, and every look self-possessed, while his voice, low in tone, had that persuasive eloquence which invariably 'moves men.'"—1832.

AN EXCERPT FROM
Memories of Great Men. . . , 1871
BY ANNA MARIA HALL

". . . He (Wordsworth) talked well in his way; with veracity, easy brevity, and force, as a wise tradesman would of his tools and workshop,—

and as no unwise one could. His voice was good, frank, and sonorous, though practically clear, distinct, and forcible, rather than melodious; the tone of him business-like, sedately confident; no discourtesy, yet no anxiety about being courteous.

A fine wholesome rusticity, fresh as his mountain breezes, sat well on the stalwart veteran, and on all he said and did. You would have said he was a usually taciturn man; glad to unlock himself to audience sympathetic and intelligent when such offered itself.

His face bore marks of much, not always peaceful, meditation; the look of it not bland or benevolent so much as close, impregnable, and hard: a man *multa tacere loquive paratus*, in a world where he had experienced no lack of contradictions as he strode along! The eyes were not very brilliant, but they had a quiet clearness; there was enough of brow, and well-shaped; rather too much of cheek ('horse face' I have heard satirists say); face of squarish shape, and decidedly longish, as I think the head itself was (its 'length' going horizontal); he was large-boned, lean, but still firm-knit, tall, and strong-looking when he stood, a right good old steel-gray figure, with rustic simplicity and dignity about him, and a vivacious strength looking through him which might have suited one of those old steel-gray markgrafs whom Henry the Fowler set up to ward the 'marches' and do battle with the heathen in a stalwart and judicious manner."

An Excerpt from
Reminiscences, 1881
by Thomas Carlyle.

NATURE POETRY

BY
WILLIAM WORDSWORTH

INFLUENCE OF NATURAL OBJECTS.

In Calling Forth and Strengthening the Imagination in Boyhood and Early Youth

Wisdom and Spirit of the universe!
Thou Soul, that art the Eternity of thought!
And giv'st to forms and images a breath
And everlasting motion! not in vain,
By day or star-light, thus from my first dawn
Of childhood didst thou intertwine for me
The passions that build up our human soul;
Not with the mean and vulgar works of Man;
But with high objects, with enduring things,
With life and nature; purifying thus
The elements of feeling and of thought,
And sanctifying by such discipline
Both pain and fear,—until we recognise
A grandeur in the beatings of the heart.

Nor was this fellowship vouchsafed to me
With stinted kindness. In November days,
When vapours rolling down the valleys made
A lonely scene more lonesome; among woods
At noon; and 'mid the calm of summer nights,
When, by the margin of the trembling lake,
Beneath the gloomy hills, homeward I went
In solitude, such intercourse was mine:
Mine was it in the fields both day and night,
And by the waters, all the summer long.
And in the frosty season, when the sun
Was set, and, visible for many a mile,
The cottage-windows through the twilight blazed,
I heeded not the summons: happy time
It was indeed for all of us; for me
It was a time of rapture! Clear and loud
The village-clock tolled six—I wheeled about,
Proud and exulting like an untired horse
That cares not for his home.—All shod with steel
We hissed along the polished ice, in games
Confederate, imitative of the chase
And woodland pleasures,—the resounding horn,
The pack loud-chiming, and the hunted hare.
So through the darkness and the cold we flew,

And not a voice was idle; with the din
Smitten, the precipices rang aloud;
The leafless trees and every icy crag
Tinkled like iron; while far-distant hills
Into the tumult sent an alien sound
Of melancholy, not unnoticed while the stars,
Eastward, were sparkling clear, and in the west
The orange sky of evening died away.

Not seldom from the uproar I retired
Into a silent bay, or sportively
Glanced sideway, leaving the tumultuous throng,
To cut across the reflex of a star;
Image, that, flying still before me, gleamed
Upon the glassy plain: and oftentimes,
When we had given our bodies to the wind,
And all the shadowy banks on either side
Came sweeping through the darkness, spinning still
The rapid line of motion, then at once
Have I, reclining back upon my heels,
Stopped short; yet still the solitary cliffs
Wheeled by me—even as if the earth had rolled
With visible motion her diurnal round!
Behind me did they stretch in solemn train,

Feebler and feebler, and I stood and watched
Till all was tranquil as a summer sea.

LINES WRITTEN WHILE SAILING IN A BOAT AT EVENING.

How richly glows the water's breast
Before us, tinged with evening hues,
While, facing thus the crimson west,
The boat her silent course pursues!
And see how dark the backward stream!
A little moment past so smiling!
And still, perhaps, with faithless gleam,
Some other loiterers beguiling.

Such views the youthful Bard allure;
But, heedless of the following gloom,
He deems their colours shall endure
Till peace go with him to the tomb.
— And let him nurse his fond deceit,
And what if he must die in sorrow!
Who would not cherish dreams so sweet,
Though grief and pain may come to-morrow?

A NIGHT-PIECE.

—The sky is overcast
With a continuous cloud of texture close,
Heavy and wan, all whitened by the Moon,
Which through that veil is indistinctly seen,
A dull, contracted circle, yielding light
So feebly spread that not a shadow falls,
Chequering the ground, from rock, plant, tree, or tower.
At length a pleasant instantaneous gleam
Startles the pensive traveller as he treads
His lonesome path, with unobserving eye
Bent earthwards; he looks up—the clouds are split
Asunder,—and above his head he sees
The clear moon, and the glory of the heavens.
There, in a black blue vault she sails along,
Followed by multitudes of stars, that, small
And sharp, and bright, along the dark abyss
Drive as she drives;—how fast they wheel away,
Yet vanish not!—the wind is in the tree,
But they are silent;—still they roll along
Immeasureably distant;—and the vault,

Built round by those white clouds, enormous clouds,
Still deepens its unfathomable depth.
At length the Vision closes; and the mind,
Not undisturbed by the delight it feels,
Which slowly settles into peaceful calm,
Is left to muse upon the solemn scene.

NUTTING.

—It seems a day
(I speak of one from many singled out)
One of those heavenly days that cannot die;
When, in the eagerness of boyish hope,
I left our cottage-threshold, sallying forth
With a huge wallet o'er my shoulders slung,
A nutting-crook in hand; and turned my steps
Tow'rd some far-distant wood, a Figure quaint,
Tricked out in proud disguise of cast-off weeds
Which for that service had been husbanded,
By exhortation of my frugal Dame—
Motley accoutrement, of power to smile
At thorns, and brakes, and brambles,—and, in truth,
More ragged than need was! O'er pathless rocks,
Through beds of matted fern, and tangled thickets,
Forcing my way, I came to one dear nook
Unvisited, where not a broken bough
Drooped with its withered leaves, ungracious sign
Of devastation; but the hazels rose
Tall and erect, with tempting clusters hung,

A virgin scene!—A little while I stood,
Breathing with such suppression of the heart
As joy delights in; and, with wise restraint
Voluptuous, fearless of a rival, eyed
The banquet;—or beneath the trees I sate
Among the flowers, and with the flowers I played;
A temper known to those, who, after long
And weary expectation, have been blest
With sudden happiness beyond all hope.
Perhaps it was a bower beneath whose leaves
The violets of five seasons re-appear
And fade, unseen by any human eye;
Where fairy water-breaks do murmur on
For ever; and I saw the sparkling foam,
And—with my cheek on one of those green stones
That, fleeced with moss, under the shady trees,
Lay round me, scattered like a flock of sheep—
I heard the murmur, and the murmuring sound,
In that sweet mood when pleasure loves to pay
Tribute to ease; and, of its joy secure,
The heart luxuriates with indifferent things,
Wasting its kindliness on stocks and stones,
And on the vacant air. Then up I rose,

And dragged to earth both branch and bough, with cras
And merciless ravage: and the shady nook
Of hazels, and the green and mossy bower,
Deformed and sullied, patiently gave up
Their quiet being: and, unless I now
Confound my present feelings with the past;
Ere from the mutilated bower I turned
Exulting, rich beyond the wealth of kings,
I felt a sense of pain when I beheld
The silent trees, and saw the intruding sky.—

Then, dearest Maiden, move along these shades
In gentleness of heart; with gentle hand
Touch—for there is a spirit in the woods.

LINES WRITTEN IN EARLY SPRING.

I heard a thousand blended notes,
While in a grove I sate reclined,
In that sweet mood when pleasant thoughts
Bring sad thoughts to the mind.

To her fair works did Nature link
The human soul that through me ran;
And much it grieved my heart to think
What man has made of man.

Through primrose tufts, in that green bower,
The periwinkle trailed its wreaths;
And 'tis my faith that every flower
Enjoys the air it breathes.

The birds around me hopped and played,
Their thoughts I cannot measure:—
But the least motion which they made
It seemed a thrill of pleasure.

The budding twigs spread out their fan,
To catch the breezy air;
And I must think, do all I can,
That there was pleasure there.

If this belief from heaven be sent,
If such be Nature's holy plan,
Have I not reason to lament
What man has made of man?

MY HEART LEAPS UP.

My heart leaps up when I behold
A rainbow in the sky:
So was it when my life began;
So is it now I am a man;
So be it when I shall grow old,
Or let me die!
The Child is father of the Man;
And I could wish my days to be
Bound each to each by natural piety.

YEW-TREES.

There is a Yew-tree, pride of Lorton Vale,
Which to this day stands single, in the midst
Of its own darkness, as it stood of yore:
Not loathe to furnish weapons for the Bands
Of Umfraville or Percy ere they marched
To Scotland's heaths; or those that crossed the sea
And drew their sounding bows at Azincour,
Perhaps at earlier Crecy, or Poictiers.
Of vast circumference and gloom profound
This solitary Tree! -a living thing
Produced too slowly ever to decay;
Of form and aspect too magnificent
To be destroyed. But worthier still of note
Are those fraternal Four of Borrowdale,
Joined in one solemn and capacious grove;
Huge trunks! -and each particular trunk a growth
Of intertwisted fibres serpentine
Up-coiling, and inveteratley convolved, -
Nor uninformed with Fantasy, and looks
That threaten the profane; -a pillared shade,

Upon whose grassless floor of red-brown hue,
By sheddings from the pining umbrage tinged
Perennially -beneath whose sable roof
Of boughs, as if for festal purpose decked
With unrejoicing berries -ghostly Shapes
May meet at noontide: Fear and trembling Hope,
Silence and Foresight, Death the Skeleton
And Time the Shadow; there to celebrate,
As in a natural temple scattered o'er
With altars undisturbed of mossy stone,
United worship; or in mute repose
To lie, and listen to the mountain flood
Murmuring from Glaramara's inmost caves.

SONNETS FROM THE RIVER DUDDON:

AFTER-THOUGHT

I thought of Thee, my partner and my guide,
As being past away.
—Vain sympathies!
For, backward, Duddon! as I cast my eyes,
I see what was, and is, and will abide;
Still glides the Stream, and shall for ever glide;
The Form remains, the Function never dies;
While we, the brave, the mighty, and the wise,
We Men, who in our morn of youth defied
The elements, must vanish;—be it so!
Enough, if something from our hands have power
To live, and act, and serve the future hour;
And if, as toward the silent tomb we go,
Through love, through hope, and faith's transcendent dower
We feel that we are greater than we know.

ADMONITION.

Intended More Particularly for the Perusal of These Who May Have Happened to be Enamoured of Some Beautiful Place of Retreat, in the Country of the Lakes.

WELL may'st thou halt—and gaze with brightening eye!
The lovely Cottage in the guardian nook
Hath stirred thee deeply; with its own dear brook,
Its own small pasture, almost its own sky!
But covet not the Abode;—forbear to sigh,
As many do, repining while they look;
Intruders—who would tear from Nature's book
This precious leaf, with harsh impiety.
Think what the home must be if it were thine,
Even thine, though few thy wants!—Roof, window, door,
The very flowers are sacred to the Poor,
The roses to the porch which they entwine:
Yea, all, that now enchants thee, from the day
On which it should be touched, would melt away.

SONNETS

BELOVED VALE! I SAID, WHEN I SHALL CON.

"Beloved Vale!" I said, "when I shall con
Those many records of my childish years,
Remembrance of myself and of my peers
Will press me down: to think of what is gone
Will be an awful thought, if life have one."
But, when into the Vale I came, no fears
Distressed me; I looked round, I shed no tears;
Deep thought, or awful vision, I had none.
By thousand petty fancies I was crost,
To see the Trees, which I had thought so tall,
Mere dwarfs; the Brooks so narrow, Fields so small.
A Juggler's Balls old Time about him tossed;
I looked, I stared, I smiled, I laughed; and all
The weight of sadness was in wonder lost.

IT IS A BEAUTEOUS EVENING, CALM AND FREE.

It is a beauteous evening, calm and free,
The holy time is quiet as a Nun
Breathless with adoration; the broad sun
Is sinking down in its tranquility;
The gentleness of heaven broods o'er the Sea;
Listen! the mighty Being is awake,
And doth with his eternal motion make
A sound like thunder—everlastingly.
Dear child! dear Girl! that walkest with me here,
If thou appear untouched by solemn thought,
Thy nature is not therefore less divine:
Thou liest in Abraham's bosom all the year;
And worshipp'st at the Temple's inner shrine,
God being with thee when we know it not.

CALM IS ALL NATURE AS A RESTING WHEEL.

Written in Very Early Youth.

Calm is all nature as a resting wheel.
The kine are couched upon the dewy grass;
The horse alone, seen dimly as I pass,
Is cropping audibly his later meal:
Dark is the ground; a slumber seems to steal
O'er vale, and mountain, and the starless sky.
Now, in this blank of things, a harmony,
Home-felt, and home-created, comes to heal

That grief for which the senses still supply
Fresh food; for only then, when memory
Is hushed, am I at rest. My Friends! restrain
Those busy cares that would allay my pain;
Oh! leave me to myself, nor let me feel
The officious touch that makes me droop again.

LINES COMPOSED A FEW MILES ABOVE TINTERN ABBEY.

On Revisiting the Banks of the Wye during a Tour. July 13, 1798

Five years have past; five summers, with the length
Of five long winters! and again I hear
These waters, rolling from their mountain-springs
With a soft inland murmur.—Once again
Do I behold these steep and lofty cliffs,
That on a wild secluded scene impress
Thoughts of more deep seclusion; and connect
The landscape with the quiet of the sky.
The day is come when I again repose
Here, under this dark sycamore, and view
These plots of cottage-ground, these orchard-tufts,
Which at this season, with their unripe fruits,
Are clad in one green hue, and lose themselves
'Mid groves and copses. Once again I see
These hedge-rows, hardly hedge-rows, little lines

Of sportive wood run wild: these pastoral farms,
Green to the very door; and wreaths of smoke
Sent up, in silence, from among the trees!
With some uncertain notice, as might seem
Of vagrant dwellers in the houseless woods,
Or of some Hermit's cave, where by his fire
The Hermit sits alone.

These beauteous forms,
Through a long absence, have not been to me
As is a landscape to a blind man's eye:
But oft, in lonely rooms, and 'mid the din
Of towns and cities, I have owed to them,
In hours of weariness, sensations sweet,
Felt in the blood, and felt along the heart;
And passing even into my purer mind
With tranquil restoration:—feelings too
Of unremembered pleasure: such, perhaps,
As have no slight or trivial influence
On that best portion of a good man's life,
His little, nameless, unremembered, acts
Of kindness and of love. Nor less, I trust,
To them I may have owed another gift,
Of aspect more sublime; that blessed mood,

In which the burthen of the mystery,
In which the heavy and the weary weight
Of all this unintelligible world,
Is lightened:—that serene and blessed mood,
In which the affections gently lead us on,—
Until, the breath of this corporeal frame
And even the motion of our human blood
Almost suspended, we are laid asleep
In body, and become a living soul:
While with an eye made quiet by the power
Of harmony, and the deep power of joy,
We see into the life of things.

If this
Be but a vain belief, yet, oh! how oft—
In darkness and amid the many shapes
Of joyless daylight; when the fretful stir
Unprofitable, and the fever of the world,
Have hung upon the beatings of my heart—
How oft, in spirit, have I turned to thee,
O sylvan Wye! thou wanderer thro' the woods,
How often has my spirit turned to thee!

And now, with gleams
of half-extinguished thought,
With many recognitions dim and faint,
And somewhat of a sad perplexity,
The picture of the mind revives again:
While here I stand, not only with the sense
Of present pleasure, but with pleasing thoughts
That in this moment there is life and food
For future years. And so I dare to hope,
Though changed, no doubt, from what I was when first
I came among these hills; when like a roe
I bounded o'er the mountains, by the sides
Of the deep rivers, and the lonely streams,
Wherever nature led: more like a man
Flying from something that he dreads, than one
Who sought the thing he loved. For nature then
(The coarser pleasures of my boyish days
And their glad animal movements all gone by)
To me was all in all.—I cannot paint
What then I was. The sounding cataract
Haunted me like a passion: the tall rock,
The mountain, and the deep and gloomy wood,
Their colours and their forms, were then to me
An appetite; a feeling and a love,

That had no need of a remoter charm,
By thought supplied, not any interest
Unborrowed from the eye.—That time is past,
And all its aching joys are now no more,
And all its dizzy raptures. Not for this
Faint I, nor mourn nor murmur; other gifts
Have followed; for such loss, I would believe,
Abundant recompense. For I have learned
To look on nature, not as in the hour
Of thoughtless youth; but hearing oftentimes
The still sad music of humanity,
Nor harsh nor grating, though of ample power
To chasten and subdue.—And I have felt
A presence that disturbs me with the joy
Of elevated thoughts; a sense sublime
Of something far more deeply interfused,
Whose dwelling is the light of setting suns,
And the round ocean and the living air,
And the blue sky, and in the mind of man:
A motion and a spirit, that impels
All thinking things, all objects of all thought,
And rolls through all things.
  Therefore am I still
A lover of the meadows and the woods

And mountains; and of all that we behold
From this green earth; of all the mighty world
Of eye, and ear,—both what they half create,
And what perceive; well pleased to recognise
In nature and the language of the sense
The anchor of my purest thoughts, the nurse,
The guide, the guardian of my heart, and soul
Of all my moral being.

Nor perchance,
If I were not thus taught, should I the more
Suffer my genial spirits to decay:
For thou art with me here upon the banks
Of this fair river; thou my dearest Friend,
My dear, dear Friend; and in thy voice I catch
The language of my former heart, and read
My former pleasures in the shooting lights
Of thy wild eyes. Oh! yet a little while
May I behold in thee what I was once,
My dear, dear Sister! and this prayer I make,
Knowing that Nature never did betray
The heart that loved her; 'tis her privilege,
Through all the years of this our life, to lead
From joy to joy: for she can so inform

The mind that is within us, so impress
With quietness and beauty, and so feed
With lofty thoughts, that neither evil tongues,
Rash judgments, nor the sneers of selfish men,
Nor greetings where no kindness is, nor all
The dreary intercourse of daily life,
Shall e'er prevail against us, or disturb
Our cheerful faith, that all which we behold
Is full of blessings. Therefore let the moon
Shine on thee in thy solitary walk;
And let the misty mountain-winds be free
To blow against thee: and, in after years,
When these wild ecstasies shall be matured
Into a sober pleasure; when thy mind
Shall be a mansion for all lovely forms,
Thy memory be as a dwelling-place
For all sweet sounds and harmonies; oh! then,
If solitude, or fear, or pain, or grief,
Should be thy portion, with what healing thoughts
Of tender joy wilt thou remember me,
And these my exhortations! Nor, perchance—
If I should be where I no more can hear
Thy voice, nor catch from thy wild eyes these gleams

Of past existence
    —wilt thou then forget
That on the banks of this delightful stream
We stood together; and that I, so long
A worshipper of Nature, hither came
Unwearied in that service: rather say
With warmer love—oh! with far deeper zeal
Of holier love. Nor wilt thou then forget,
That after many wanderings, many years
Of absence, these steep woods and lofty cliffs,
And this green pastoral landscape, were to me
More dear, both for themselves and for thy sake!

ODE

Intimations of Immortality from Recollections of Early Childhood

There was a time when meadow, grove, and stream,
The earth, and every common sight,
To me did seem
Apparelled in celestial light,
The glory and the freshness of a dream.
It is not now as it hath been of yore;—
Turn wheresoe'er I may,
By night or day.
The things which I have seen I now can see no more.

The Rainbow comes and goes,
And lovely is the Rose,
The Moon doth with delight
Look round her when the heavens are bare,
Waters on a starry night
Are beautiful and fair;

The sunshine is a glorious birth;
But yet I know, where'er I go,
That there hath past away a glory from the earth.

Now, while the birds thus sing a joyous song,
And while the young lambs bound
As to the tabor's sound,
To me alone there came a thought of grief:
A timely utterance gave that thought relief,
And I again am strong:
The cataracts blow their trumpets from the steep;
No more shall grief of mine the season wrong;
I hear the Echoes through the mountains throng,
The Winds come to me from the fields of sleep,
And all the earth is gay;
Land and sea
Give themselves up to jollity,
And with the heart of May
Doth every Beast keep holiday;—
Thou Child of Joy,
Shout round me, let me hear thy shouts,
thou happy Shepherd-boy.

Ye blessèd creatures, I have heard the call
Ye to each other make; I see
The heavens laugh with you in your jubilee;
My heart is at your festival,
My head hath its coronal,
The fulness of your bliss, I feel—I feel it all.
Oh evil day! if I were sullen
While Earth herself is adorning,
This sweet May-morning,
And the Children are culling
On every side,
In a thousand valleys far and wide,
Fresh flowers; while the sun shines warm,
And the Babe leaps up on his Mother's arm:—
I hear, I hear, with joy I hear!
—But there's a Tree, of many, one,
A single field which I have looked upon,
Both of them speak of something that is gone;
The Pansy at my feet
Doth the same tale repeat:
Whither is fled the visionary gleam?
Where is it now, the glory and the dream?

Our birth is but a sleep and a forgetting:
The Soul that rises with us, our life's Star,
Hath had elsewhere its setting,
And cometh from afar:
Not in entire forgetfulness,
And not in utter nakedness,
But trailing clouds of glory do we come
From God, who is our home:
Heaven lies about us in our infancy!
Shades of the prison-house begin to close
Upon the growing Boy,
But he beholds the light, and whence it flows,
He sees it in his joy;
The Youth, who daily farther from the east
Must travel, still is Nature's Priest,
And by the vision splendid
Is on his way attended;
At length the Man perceives it die away,
And fade into the light of common day.

Earth fills her lap with pleasures of her own;
Yearnings she hath in her own natural kind,
And, even with something of a Mother's mind,
And no unworthy aim,

The homely Nurse doth all she can
To make her Foster-child, her Inmate Man,
Forget the glories he hath known,
And that imperial palace whence he came.

Behold the Child among his new-born blisses,
A six years' Darling of a pigmy size!
See, where 'mid work of his own hand he lies,
Fretted by sallies of his mother's kisses,
With light upon him from his father's eyes!
See, at his feet, some little plan or chart,
Some fragment from his dream of human life,
Shaped by himself with newly-learn{e}d art
A wedding or a festival,
A mourning or a funeral;
And this hath now his heart,
And unto this he frames his song:
Then will he fit his tongue
To dialogues of business, love, or strife;
But it will not be long
Ere this be thrown aside,
And with new joy and pride
The little Actor cons another part;
Filling from time to time his "humorous stage"

With all the Persons, down to palsied Age,
That Life brings with her in her equipage;
As if his whole vocation
Were endless imitation.

Thou, whose exterior semblance doth belie
Thy Soul's immensity;
Thou best Philosopher, who yet dost keep
Thy heritage, thou Eye among the blind,
That, deaf and silent, read'st the eternal deep,
Haunted for ever by the eternal mind,—
Mighty Prophet! Seer blest!
On whom those truths do rest,
Which we are toiling all our lives to find,
In darkness lost, the darkness of the grave;
Thou, over whom thy Immortality
Broods like the Day, a Master o'er a Slave,
A Presence which is not to be put by;
Thou little Child, yet glorious in the might
Of heaven-born freedom on thy being's height,
Why with such earnest pains dost thou provoke
The years to bring the inevitable yoke,
Thus blindly with thy blessedness at strife?
Full soon thy Soul shall have her earthly freight,

And custom lie upon thee with a weight,
Heavy as frost, and deep almost as life!

O joy! that in our embers
Is something that doth live,
That Nature yet remembers
What was so fugitive!
The thought of our past years in me doth breed
Perpetual benediction: not indeed
For that which is most worthy to be blest;
Delight and liberty, the simple creed
Of Childhood, whether busy or at rest,
With new-fledged hope still fluttering in his breast:—
Not for these I raise
The song of thanks and praise
But for those obstinate questionings
Of sense and outward things,
Fallings from us, vanishings;
Blank misgivings of a Creature
Moving about in worlds not realised,
High instincts before which our mortal Nature
Did tremble like a guilty thing surprised:
But for those first affections,
Those shadowy recollections,

Which, be they what they may
Are yet the fountain-light of all our day,
Are yet a master-light of all our seeing;
Uphold us, cherish, and have power to make
Our noisy years seem moments in the being
Of the eternal Silence: truths that wake,
To perish never;
Which neither listlessness, nor mad endeavour,
Nor Man nor Boy,
Nor all that is at enmity with joy,
Can utterly abolish or destroy!
Hence in a season of calm weather
Though inland far we be,
Our Souls have sight of that immortal sea
Which brought us hither,
Can in a moment travel thither,
And see the Children sport upon the shore,
And hear the mighty waters rolling evermore.

Then sing, ye Birds, sing, sing a joyous song!
And let the young Lambs bound
As to the tabor's sound!
We in thought will join your throng,
Ye that pipe and ye that play,

Ye that through your hearts to-day
Feel the gladness of the May!
What though the radiance which was once so bright
Be now for ever taken from my sight,
Though nothing can bring back the hour
Of splendour in the grass, of glory in the flower;
We will grieve not, rather find
Strength in what remains behind;
In the primal sympathy
Which having been must ever be;
In the soothing thoughts that spring
Out of human suffering;
In the faith that looks through death,
In years that bring the philosophic mind.
And O, ye Fountains, Meadows, Hills, and Groves,
Forebode not any severing of our loves!
Yet in my heart of hearts I feel your might;
I only have relinquished one delight
To live beneath your more habitual sway.
I love the Brooks which down their channels fret,
Even more than when I tripped lightly as they;
The innocent brightness of a new-born Day
Is lovely yet;
The Clouds that gather round the setting sun

Do take a sober colouring from an eye
That hath kept watch o'er man's mortality;
Another race hath been, and other palms are won.
Thanks to the human heart by which we live,
Thanks to its tenderness, its joys, and fears,
To me the meanest flower that blows can give
Thoughts that do often lie too deep for tears

IT WAS AN APRIL MORNING:

FRESH AND CLEAR.

It was an April morning: fresh and clear
The Rivulet, delighting in its strength,
Ran with a young man's speed; and yet the voice
Of waters which the winter had supplied
Was softened down into a vernal tone.
The spirit of enjoyment and desire,
And hopes and wishes, from all living things
Went circling, like a multitude of sounds.
The budding groves seemed eager to urge on
The steps of June; as if their various hues
Were only hindrances that stood between
Them and their object: but, meanwhile, prevailed
Such an entire contentment in the air
That every naked ash, and tardy tree
Yet leafless, showed as if the countenance
With which it looked on this delightful day
Were native to the summer.—Up the brook

I roamed in the confusion of my heart,
Alive to all things and forgetting all.
At length I to a sudden turning came
In this continuous glen, where down a rock
The Stream, so ardent in its course before,
Sent forth such sallies of glad sound, that all
Which I till then had heard, appeared the voice
Of common pleasure: beast and bird, the lamb,
The shepherd's dog, the linnet and the thrush
Vied with this waterfall, and made a song,
Which, while I listened, seemed like the wild growth
Or like some natural produce of the air,
That could not cease to be. Green leaves were here;
But 'twas the foliage of the rocks—the birch,
The yew, the holly, and the bright green thorn,
With hanging islands of resplendent furze:
And, on a summit, distant a short space,
By any who should look beyond the dell,
A single mountain-cottage might be seen.
I gazed and gazed, and to myself I said,
'Our thoughts at least are ours; and this wild nook,
My EMMA, I will dedicate to thee.'
—Soon did the spot become my other home,
My dwelling, and my out-of-doors abode.

And, of the Shepherds who have seen me there,
To whom I sometimes in our idle talk
Have told this fancy, two or three, perhaps,
Years after we are gone and in our graves,
When they have cause to speak of this wild place,
May call it by the name of EMMA's DELL.

THERE IS AN EMINENCE.

There is an Eminence,—of these our hills
The last that parleys with the setting sun.
We can behold it from our Orchard-seat;
And, when at evening we pursue our walk
Along the public way, this Cliff, so high
Above us, and so distant in its height,
Is visible; and often seems to send
Its own deep quiet to restore our hearts.
The meteors make of it a favourite haunt:
The star of Jove, so beautiful and large
In the mid heavens, is never half so fair
As when he shines above it. 'Tis in truth
The loneliest place we have among the clouds.
And She who dwells with me, whom 1 have loved
With such communion, that no place on earth
Can ever be a solitude to me,
Hath to this lonely summit given my Name.

A narrow girdle of rough stones and crags,
A rude and natural causeway, interposed
Between the water and a winding slope
Of copse and thicket, leaves the eastern shore
Of Grasmere safe in its own privacy:
And there myself and two beloved Friends,
One calm September morning, ere the mist
Had altogether yielded to the sun,
Sauntered on this retired and difficult way.
—Ill suits the road with one in haste; but we
Played with our time; and, as we strolled along,
It was our occupation to observe
Such objects as the waves had tossed ashore—
Feather, or leaf, or weed, or withered bough,
Each on the other heaped, along the line
Of the dry wreck. And, in our vacant mood,
Not seldom did we stop to watch some tuft
Of dandelion seed or thistle's beard,
That skimmed the surface of the dead calm lake,
Suddenly halting now—a lifeless stand!
And starting off again with freak as sudden;
In all its sportive wanderings, all the while,
Making report of an invisible breeze
That was its wings, its chariot, and its horse,

Its playmate, rather say, its moving soul.
—And often, trifling with a privilege
Alike indulged to all, we paused, one now,
And now the other, to point out, perchance
To pluck, some flower or water-weed, too fair
Either to be divided from the place
On which it grew, or to be left alone
To its own beauty. Many such there are,
Fair ferns and flowers, and chiefly that tall fern,
So stately, of the queen Osmunda named;
Plant lovelier, in its own retired abode
On Grasmere's beach, than Naiad by the side
Of Grecian brook, or Lady of the Mere,
Sole-sitting by the shores of old romance.
—So fared we that bright morning: from the fields
Meanwhile, a noise was heard, the busy mirth
Of reapers, men and women, boys and girls.
Delighted much to listen to those sounds,
And feeding thus our fancies, we advanced
Along the indented shore; when suddenly,
Through a thin veil of glittering haze was seen
Before us, on a point of jutting land,
The tall and upright figure of a Man
Attired in peasant's garb, who stood alone,

Angling beside the margin of the lake.
'Improvident and reckless,' we exclaimed,
'The Man must be, who thus can lose a day
Of the mid harvest, when the labourer's hire
Is ample, and some little might be stored
Wherewith to cheer him in the winter time.'
Thus talking of that Peasant, we approached
Close to the spot where with his rod and line
He stood alone; whereat he turned his head
To greet us—and we saw a Mam worn down
By sickness, gaunt and lean, with sunken cheeks
And wasted limbs, his legs so long and lean
That for my single self I looked at them,
Forgetful of the body they sustained.—
Too weak to labour in the harvest field,
The Man was using his best skill to gain
A pittance from the dead unfeeling lake
That knew not of his wants. I will not say
What thoughts immediately were ours, nor how
The happy idleness of that sweet morn,
With all its lovely images, was changed
To serious musing and to self-reproach.
Nor did we fail to see within ourselves
What need there is to be reserved in speech,

And temper all our thoughts with charity.
—Therefore, unwilling to forget that day,
My Friend, Myself, and She who then received
The same admonishment, have called the place
By a memorial name, uncouth indeed
As e'er by mariner was given to bay
Or foreland, on a new-discovered coast;
And POINT RASH-JUDGMENT is the name it bears.

ON THE BANKS OF A ROCKY STREAM.

Behold an emblem of our human mind
Crowded with thoughts that need a settled home,
Yet, like to eddying balls of foam
Within this whirlpool, they each other chase
Round and round, and neither find
An outlet nor a resting-place!
Stranger, if such disquietude be thine,
Fall on thy knees and sue for help divine.

TO THE CLOUDS.

Army of Clouds! ye winged Hosts in troops
Ascending from behind the motionless brow
Of that tall rock, as from a hidden world,
Oh whither with such eagerness of speed?
What seek ye, or what shun ye? of the gale
Companions, fear ye to be left behind,
Or racing o'er your blue ethereal field
Contend ye with each other? of the sea
Children, thus post ye over vale and height
To sink upon your's mother's lap and rest?
Or were ye rightlier hailed, when first mine eyes
Beheld in your impetuous march the likeness
Of a wide army pressing on to meet
Or overtake some unknown enemy?
But your smooth motions suit a peaceful aim;
And Fancy, not less aptly pleased, compares
Your squadrons to an endless flight of birds
Aerial, upon due migration bound
To milder climes; or rather do ye urge
In caravan your hasty pilgrimage

To pause at last on more aspiring heights
Than these, and utter your devotion there
With thunderous voice? Or are ye jubilant,
And would ye, tracking your proud lord the Sun,
Be present at his setting; or the pomp
Of Persian mornings would ye fill, and stand
Poising your splendours high above the heads
Of worshipers kneeling to their up-risen God?
Whence, whence, ye Clouds! this eagerness of speed?
Speak, silent creatures. They are gone, are fled,
Buried together in yon gloomy mass
That loads the middle heaven; and clear and bright
And vacant doth the region which they thronged
Appear; a calm descent of sky conducting
Down to the unapproachable abyss,
Down to that hidden gulf from which they rose
To vanish, fleet as days and months and years,
Fleet as the generations of mankind,
Power, glory, empire, as the world itself,
The lingering world, when time hath ceased to be.
But the winds roar, shaking the rooted trees,
And see! a bright precursor to a train
Perchance as numerous, overpeers the rock
That sullenly refuses to partake

Of the wild impulse. From a fount of life
Invisible, the long procession moves
Luminous or gloomy, welcome to the vale
Which they are entering, welcome to mine eye
That sees them, to my soul that owns in them,
And in the bosom of the firmament
O'er which they move, wherein they are contained,
A type of her capacious self and all
Her restless progeny.

A humble walk
Here is my body doomed to tread, this path,
A little hoary line and faintly traced,
Work, shall we call it, of the shepherd's foot
Or of his flock? joint vestige of them both.
I pace it unrepining, for my thoughts
Admit no bondage and my words have wings.
Where is the Orphean lyre, or Druid harp,
To accompany the verse? The mountain blast
Shall be our 'hand' of music; he shall sweep
The rocks, and quivering trees, and billowy lake,
And search the fibres of the caves, and they
Shall answer, for our song is of the Clouds
And the wind loves them; and the gentle gales

Which by their aid re-clothe the naked lawn
With annual verdure, and revive the woods,
And moisten the parched lips of thirsty flowers
Love them; and every idle breeze of air
Bends to the favourite burthen. Moon and stars
Keep their most solemn vigils when the Clouds
Watch also, shifting peaceably their place
Like bands of ministering Spirits, or when they lie,
As if some Protean art the change had wrought,
In listless quiet o'er the ethereal deep
Scattered, a Cyclades of various shapes
And all degrees of beauty. O ye Lightnings!
Ye are their perilous offspring; and the Sun
Source inexhaustible of life and joy,
And type of man's far-darting reason, therefore
In old time worshiped as the god of verse,
A blazing intellectual deity
Loves his own glory in their looks, and showers
Upon that unsubstantial brotherhood
Visions with all but beatific light
Enriched too transient were they not renewed
From age to age, and did not, while we gaze
In silent rapture, credulous desire
Nourish the hope that memory lacks not power

To keep the treasure unimpaired. Vain thought!
Yet why repine, created as we are
For joy and rest, albeit to find them only
Lodged in the bosom of eternal things?

TO THE MOON.

Wanderer! that stoop'st so low, and com'st so near
To human life's unsettled atmosphere;
Who lov'st with Night and Silence to partake,
So might it seem, the cares of them that wake;
And, through the cottage-lattice softly peeping,
Dost shield from harm the humblest of the sleeping;
What pleasure once encompassed those sweet names
Which yet in thy behalf the Poet claims,
An idolizing dreamer as of yore! —
I slight them all; and, on this sea-beat shore
Sole-sitting, only can to thoughts attend
That bid me hail thee as the Sailor 's FRIEND ;
So call thee for heaven's grace through thee made known
By confidence supplied and mercy shown,
When not a twinkling star or beacon's light
Abates the perils of a stormy night;
And for less obvious benefits, that find
Their way, with thy pure help, to heart and mind;
Both for the adventurer starting in life's prime;
And veteran ranging round from clime to clime,

Long-baffled hope's slow fever in his veins,
And wounds and weakness oft his labour's sole remains.

The aspiring Mountains and the winding Streams,
Empress of Night! are gladdened by thy beams;
A look of thine the wilderness pervades,
And penetrates the forest's inmost shades;
Thou, chequering peaceably the minster's gloom,
Guid'st the pale Mourner to the lost one's tomb;
Canst reach the Prisoner — to his grated cell
Welcome, though silent and intangible! —
And lives there one, of all that come and go
On the great waters toiling to and fro,
One, who has watched thee at some quiet hour
Enthroned aloft in undisputed power,
Or crossed by vapoury streaks and clouds that move
Catching the lustre they in part reprove —
Nor sometimes felt a fitness in thy sway
To call up thoughts that shun the glare of day,
And make the serious happier than the gay?

Yes, lovely Moon! if thou so mildly bright
Dost rouse, yet surely in thy own despite,
To fiercer mood the frenzy-stricken brain,

Let me a compensating faith maintain;
That there's a sensitive, a tender, part
Which thou canst touch in every human heart,
For healing and composure. — But, as least
And mightiest billows ever have confessed
Thy domination; as the whole vast Sea
Feels through her lowest depths thy sovereignty;
So shines that countenance with especial grace
On them who urge the keel her plains to trace
Furrowing its way right onward. The most rude,
Cut off from home and country, may have stood —
Even till long gazing hath bedimmed his eye,
Or the mute rapture ended in a sigh —
Touched by accordance of thy placid cheer,
With some internal lights to memory dear,
Or fancies stealing forth to soothe the breast
Tired with its daily share of earth's unrest, —
Gentle awakenings, visitations meek;
A kindly influence whereof few will speak,
Though it can wet with tears the hardiest cheek.

And when thy beauty in the shadowy cave
Is hidden, buried in its monthly grave;
Then, while the Sailor, 'mid an open sea

Swept by a favouring wind that leaves thought free,
Paces the deck — no star perhaps in sight,
And nothing save the moving ship's own light
To cheer the long dark hours of vacant night —
Oft with his musings does thy image blend,
In his mind's eye thy crescent horns ascend,
And thou art still, O Moon, that Sailor 's FRIEND !

COMPOSED AT RYDAL ON MAY MORNING.

If with old love of you, dear Hills! I share
New love of many a rival image brought
From far, forgive the wanderings of my thought:
Nor art thou wronged, sweet May! when I compare
Thy present birth-morn with thy last, so fair,
So rich to me in favours. For my lot
Then was, within the famed Egerian Grot
To sit and muse, fanned by its dewy air
Mingling with thy soft breath! That morning too,
Warblers I heard their joy unbosoming
Amid the sunny, shadowy, Coliseum;
Heard them, unchecked by aught of saddening hue,
For victories there won by flower-crowned Spring,
Chant in full choir their innocent Te Deum.

COMPOSED BY THE SEA-SHORE.

What mischief cleaves to unsubdued regret,
How fancy sickens by vague hopes beset;
How baffled projects on the spirit prey,
And fruitless wishes eat the heart away,
The Sailor knows; he best, whose lot is cast
On the relentless sea that holds him fast
On chance dependent, and the fickle star
Of power, through long and melancholy war.
O sad it is, in sight of foreign shores,
Daily to think on old familiar doors,
Hearths loved in childhood, and ancestral floors;
Or, tossed about along a waste of foam,
To ruminate on that delightful home
Which with the dear Betrothed 'was' to come;
Or came and was and is, yet meets the eye
Never but in the world of memory;
Or in a dream recalled, whose smoothest range
Is crossed by knowledge, or by dread, of change,
And if not so, whose perfect joy makes sleep

A thing too bright for breathing man to keep.
Hail to the virtues which that perilous life
Extracts from Nature's elemental strife;
And welcome glory won in battles fought
As bravely as the foe was keenly sought.
But to each gallant Captain and his crew
A less imperious sympathy is due,
Such as my verse now yields, while moonbeams play
On the mute sea in this unruffled bay;
Such as will promptly flow from every breast,
Where good men, disappointed in the quest
Of wealth and power and honours, long for rest;
Or, having known the splendours of success,
Sigh for the obscurities of happiness.

BIBLIOGRAPHY

INFLUENCE OF NATURAL OBJECTS.

Written as part of *The Prelude*, 1850, but first published in *The Friend - A Series of Essays* by Samuel Taylor, 1812.

LINES WRITTEN WHILE SAILING IN A BOAT AT EVENING.

Published in *Lyrical Ballads*, 1798. The title of the poem in 1798, when it consisted of five stanzas, was *Lines written near Richmond, upon the Thames, at Evening*. When, in the edition of 1800, it was divided, the title of the first part was, *Lines written when sailing in a Boat at Evening*; that of the second part was *Lines written near Richmond upon the Thames.* From 1815 to 1843, both poems were placed by Wordsworth among those "of Sentiment and Reflection." In 1845 they were transferred to "Poems written in Youth.

A NIGHT-PIECE.

First Published in *Poems, Volume I,* 1815.

NUTTING.

First Published in *Lyrical Ballads, Volume II*, 1800.

LINES WRITTEN IN EARLY SPRING.

First Published in *Lyrical Ballads, First Edition, 1798.*

MY HEART LEAPS UP.

First published in *Poems, in Two Volumes*, 1807.

YEW-TREES.

Written in 1803, first published in *Poems, Volume I*, 1815 and is also one of the *Poems of the Imagination* Series.

SONNETS FROM THE RIVER DUDDON: AFTER-THOUGHT

First published in *The River Duddon, a Series of Sonnets*, 1820.

ADMONITION.

Composed in 1806 and classed among the *Miscellaneous Sonnets*, published in *Poems, Volume II*, 1815.

SONNETS - BELOVED VALE! I SAID, WHEN I SHALL CON.

Composed in 1806 and published in *Poems, in Two Volumes,* 1807 as No. 15 of the *Miscellaneous Sonnets.*

IT IS A BEAUTEOUS EVENING, CALM AND FREE.

Composed in August, 1802 and published in *Poems, in Two Volumes,* 1807 as No. 19 of the *Miscellaneous Sonnets.*

CALM IS ALL NATURE AS A RESTING WHEEL.

Composed in 1786, Published in *Poems, in Two Volumes,* 1807 as No. 13 of the *Miscellaneous Sonnets.*

LINES COMPOSED A FEW MILES ABOVE TINTERN ABBEY.

First published in *Lyrical Ballads, First Edition, 1798.*

ODE - INTIMATIONS OF IMMORTALITY.

Completed in 1804 and first published in *Poems, in Two Volumes,* 1807.

IT WAS AN APRIL MORNING: FRESH AND CLEAR.

First published in *Lyrical Ballads, Volume II*, 1800.

THERE IS AN EMINENCE.

First published in *Lyrical Ballads, Volume II*, 1800.

ON THE BANKS OF A ROCKY STREAM.

First published in *The River Duddon, a Series of Sonnets*, 1820.

TO THE CLOUDS.

First published in *Poems Chiefly of Early and Late Years*, 1842 and is also included in the *Poems of Imagination* Series.

TO THE MOON.

Composed in 1835 and published in *The Poetical Works of William Wordsworth, Volume VIII*, 1896. Is part of the *Evening Voluntaries* Series.

COMPOSED AT RYDAL ON MAY MORNING.

Composed in May, 1838. This sonnet was first published in the *Volume of Collected Sonnets* in 1838. In 1842 it was classed among the *Miscellaneous Sonnets*; but in 1845 it was transferred to the *Memorials of a Tour in Italy*, 1837.

COMPOSED BY THE SEASHORE.

Composed in 1834 and published in *The Poetical Works of William Wordsworth, Volume VII,* 1896. Is part of the *Evening Voluntaries* Series.